Halfway To The Stars

Sarah Gate

To women everywhere and the men who fight for them.
To the animals. We see you. We hear you.
To my mamma.
To my sister.

ISBN 978-1-5272-4218-0
Illustrations by Angelo R. (Insta. @angelorstudio)

Raise us.

Raise boys
who treat women
the way you wish your father treated your mother

and girls
as strong as
you wish your mother was.

Melissa.

You are both me
and not me.

My sister.

The better bits of what I am and all I want to be.

The 'not all men' men.

When he comes for you again, which he will, my timid friend, take your knee and jam it in the place that seeks you out.

When his hands grab at your waist, or force an uninvited embrace, take your hand and rip his plans and parts to little pieces.

When he commands you look at him, or gift him a foreboding grin, take your teeth and mark your grief across his sickening skin.

When his lips search hungrily, despite your sobs and whines and weeping, close your eyes and wonder where the 'not all men' men are.

<u>Earthling.</u>

I'll find my home on undiscovered hills
and on nondescript seabeds.
In over-trekked forests and frequented beaches.
In caves both bashful and brazen.

I'll make my bed on cold, hard rocks unworthy of a
second glance.
I'll cover myself with sand softer than silk
and bathe in waterfalls millions of years in the
making.

I'll rest my head wherever it sinks and bask in
unfathomable familiarity.
"Hello mother," I'll say. "I'm back."

"I've been waiting for you," the Earth will whisper.
"Welcome home, my love."

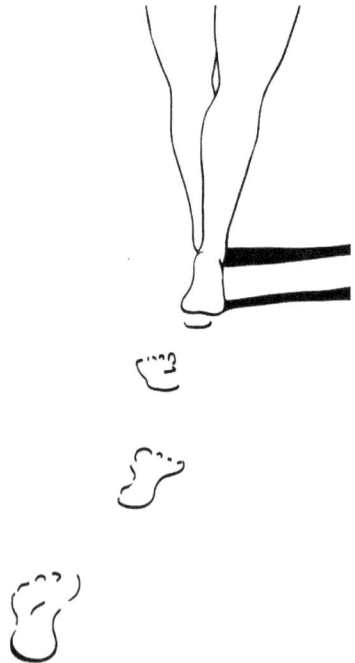

<u>My darling.</u>

Oh darling,
don't you know
that you were always mine?

How could you not?

Weren't you yearning for my touch
even when she ran her fingers over you?

Weren't you longing to devour me
even as she lapped you up?

Weren't you calling my name
even as she gasped yours?

Have you missed me?
Your home is in my heart.
You know that already.

Come back to me.
You'll find the missing piece of you.
The part you seek when you plough yourself into
others.
It's here. Right here.
Waiting for you.

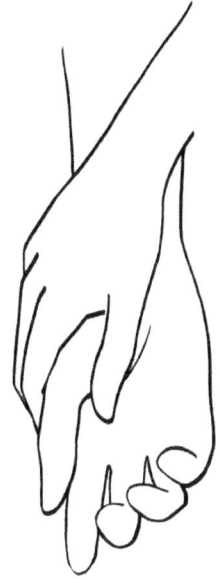

Cinders.

Seeing you crash is like watching somebody rip up a
book, or a cathedral I never knew I cared about burn
to the ground.
I shouldn't be sad, you are just a thing to me, but
I am.
You're beautiful.
So beautiful.
You make people feel something they cannot explain.
They taste the ash in their mouths when you set
yourself alight.
It coats their teeth and blocks their windpipes.
They choke whilst they watch you scorch.
You fill their nostrils whilst you sit beside them
and sputter.
They fidget uncomfortably, take out their money and
try to make it better, but paper is the last thing
you need.
You sizzle so viciously that you would melt nickel.
You are helpless. It is hopeless.
And there is nothing that anyone can do,
though they try,
but brace themselves to watch you burn again and
again and again.

<u>Don't leave.</u>

She is not someone,
to leave and then love.

If you're hoping your absence will grow her heart
it won't.

If you think your games will foster her interest
they will not.

She is afraid, but she is strong.

Your flitty fingers and thirstlessness will urge her
elsewhere.

So nudge aside her ego instead
with gentle and regular words.

Smash the silence she expects
with a brazeness that makes you blush.

Chase her.

Be brave.
Make her laugh.
Tell her truths.
Share the deepest secrets of your soul.

But don't leave.
Never leave.

For she will gouge you shamelessly
forever from her heart.

<u>My fanciful lover.</u>

You'll never be mine outside of my mind,
and that's alright with me.

I long too strongly to own you.

I am quite sure that you are sweeter than a spring
blue sky,
but skies split sometimes
and I already know that I couldn't weather the
thunder.

And if you were to love me with any less strength
than that of a raging sea,
it would destroy me.

If you did not cast your body onto mine and burst
like a volcano,
it would tear my world apart.

So stay in my head, where I'm safe from your wide-
eyed indifference.

Live in my imagination.

Save me the bitterness of your disinterest.

And I'll plead with a star to
 the wonder of your universe far from me.

My fanciful lover, my fictional friend, may we never
meet beyond fantasy.

<u>Quiet, man.</u>

Close your mouth, man.
You are he who made me.

I'll scream the pain of a million tortured souls
straight into your face,
with the voice you claim you gave me
only when it speaks the things you want to hear.

"She's mine," you declare. "Made by me."

And how much it would hurt you to know that I never
belonged to you.

How bitterly happy that makes me.

I belong to the vulnerable,
the needy,
the voiceless,
the desperate.

They taste like lemons.

I throw myself at their feet.
hold out the heart you made
and plead with them to take it.

They smell like citrus.

Shut your mouth, man.
You are he who made me.

And this mouth you made by mistake will one day
swallow you whole.

Wrestling.

If he loves you,
you will never have to wrestle him for his heart.

He will gouge it from his chest and hand it to you
himself.

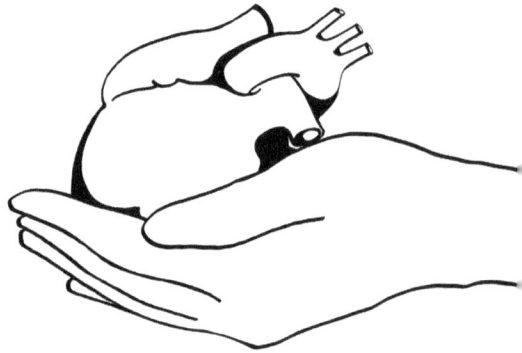

Blue eyes.

I'll never know why
boys with blue eyes
are not my thing.

Unless the eyes are blue and belong to you.

Never more than shit.

When you rip the flesh between your teeth
how is it that you cannot see
the eyes of those whose skin you eat?

And when the juice drips down your chin
how is it that you have not tasted
the blood of he whose life you wasted?

Imagine now your own sweet self,
ground up with blades and knives and shears,
and fed to those who could live without
your fat and eyes and hooves and ears.

Think too of those born of your loins,
ripped from your arms,
torn from themselves,
to satisfy the casual hunger
of those who won't eat something else.

Tell me how you do not care,
when with each gnash of your teeth,
each mouthful,
each crunch and chew,
each swallow,
each happy and grabby wipe at your satisfied lips,
you eat from the flesh of he or she
who wanted to live
passing them through your greedy guts
and turning them to shit.

Oh woman!

Oh woman!, they cry. Don't you read?
Don't you vote?
Or bear children?
Or save yourself and dress with respect?

Oh woman!, they implore. You can talk.
But not too much.
And not too loud.
And not too truthfully, please.

Oh woman!, they scream. Don't you hear me?
You're not listening.
Not understanding.
And you expect to know too much now.

Oh woman!, they bang. You are hysterical.
Just let us hold you.
Touch you.
Do as we have always done.

Oh woman!, they sigh. Won't you just give up?
Shut your mouth?
Ignore injustice?
And tell us we have done enough.

The problem, we've decided, oh woman!, is not us.

It is you, oh woman!

Oh women, it is you.

Slaves.

They tie your hands the moment you are born.
Force-feed you candy colours and money making brain
vomit.
They tell you you're free, knot your blindfold at
the back and whisper with sweetness.

"No need to think, dear. We can do that for you."

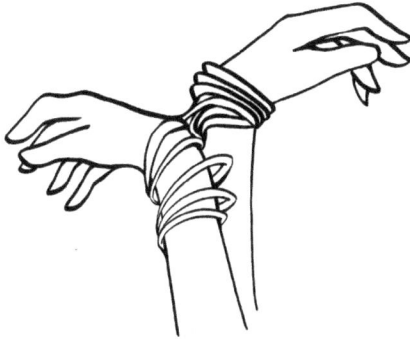

No, no, no.

Men are not therapy, darling, and you are no
patient.
Nor are you rehabilitation for boys who do not know
themselves.

Men are not superheroes, my love, and you are no
damsel in distress.
The only wicked witch you know is lodged inside your
heart.

<u>You're different.</u>

They tell you you're different and it makes you feel strange.

But you are not driven by the desire to be unlike anybody else. Or to be the same.

It's just that you are.

They tell you that they wish they could be more like you,
that they're proud of who you turned into;
intrigued by you,
inspired,
but you wish by the night that you weren't so complicated.
That your head was not a web of worry and wonderment and bewilderment, and that you could talk more about the things on TV.
About mortgages and weddings and children who hate you for putting them to bed.
That you might have a favourite holiday resort in Tenerife,
a best restaurant
and care about the colour of curtains.

That is fine, but it is not you.
That is hard, but undeniably true.

You are not lost, you are wandering.
Not confused, but wondering.
Keep going, heartbreaker. World saver.
Feet like yours pave paths through meadows and set souls alight.

You're going to be okay, my friend.
You're going to be alright.

Iris.

My mouth is a barrier to my heart.
Listen to my eyes, instead.
I implore my tongue to stop shuddering.
Beg you with wide eyes not to judge me by my shy
lips and the things they say.

They are fat and boastful.
Stupid.
Unapologetic.
Arrogant.

My heart is afraid and she flitters and flaps.
Lets my lips do the talking, though she knows she
should not.

For they say things
only to protect her,
the way my mother does.
And they ruin things
by accident
the way a father might.
But my eyes tell the truth.
"Hello.
Thank you for listening.
I'm sorry about lips.
She does not mean the things she says.
She's nervous, you see.
Forgive her.
Forgive me."

Listen. Look. You'll see it. You'll hear it.
If you want to.
It's all there. It's all there in my eyes.

<u>Kiss me with purpose.</u>

Kiss me with purpose.
Tear my legs apart and cast your knee deliciously
between my thighs.

Put your hands where I want them.
No, not there. Not yet.
But there. Yes. Right there.

Press me into something.
A bed. A wall. The floor.
Kiss me in all the right places.
My lips. My neck. My chest.

Pull my hair.
Harder. Harder.
Harder.
Make noise.
Gasp. Moan. Talk.
Laugh if you want to.

Stare into my eyes,
or bury your face in
my hair.

Then go.
Just go.
Fill me with the best
of yourself.
Again. And again. And
again.
Bite me.
Scratch me.
Devour me.
Exhaust me.

Then kiss me.
Kiss me with purpose.

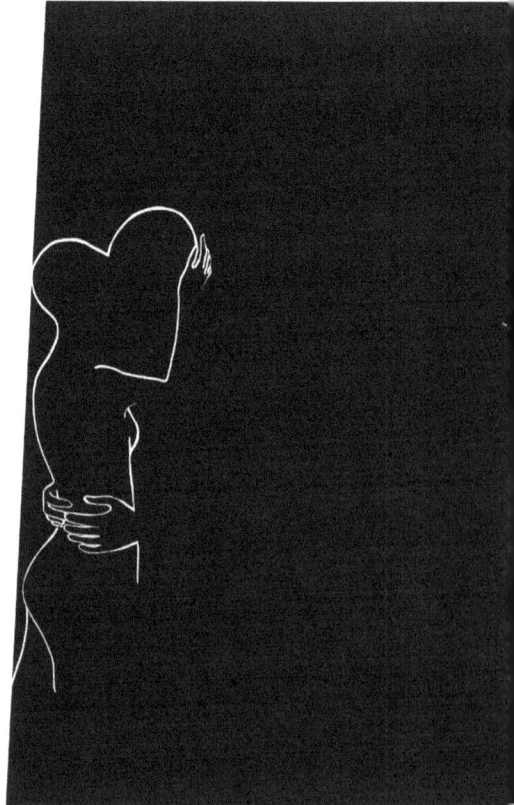

Pankhurst's damsel.

And aren't you brave,
to love someone like me?
Someone so sad and incomplete.

Do not try to fix me.

My darling,
your parts, however impressive, cannot make me
whole.
Your skill will not complete me.
I would never let it.

I am not your project.
Not yours to save
or fix.
If you are looking for a damsel
you will not find her here.

Beware, gentle boy.

I'll drown you,
smother you,
strangle you until you're torn.

And it will build me up.

But you're brave, you say.
You tell me, with glee, that you are not afraid.
You should be.

I'll cover you with ripped up pieces of me.
I'll pull you apart,
limb from limb.
I'll beat you with my broken bits
until you're broken, too.

L.

You're a bad decision hiding behind a smile
and I see you,
the real you,
and your complicated brain and every wound you have.
It should make me afraid
but I'll fall anyway
because it is not your smile I am powerless to
resist,
it's the secrets you hide behind it
and the broken bits of you the other girls don't
care to see.

<u>Halfway to the stars.</u>

I'm a dreamer.
A doer.
A poet.
A writer.
I'm halfway to the stars.

I don't know what I want but I know what I don't
want. Isn't that more important?

I'm an optimist.
A thinker.
A creative.
A character.
My soul sits on the moon.

I don't know who I am but I know who I'm not. Isn't
that almost the same?

Mike.

You take on too much, my love.
Don't you see that the world is not yours to
correct?
To make clean?
That we are not sitting on your shoulders, waiting
to be saved?
You, my dear, are not the problem.
You're wonderful.
Different except in the way that you hate yourself.

So stand as tall as you are and don't stoop.
Command the change you are seeking with your white
man's voice.
Let go of the worry the way women do.
The way all tortured souls dismiss torment.
The way we have to or else we would die.
Take comfort in your own company.
Stop searching for soft, slender fingers and caress
yourself instead.
We cannot heal you,
any more than you can heal yourself.
So surrender, my friend. Stay haunted.
You are possessed by the most beautiful rage.
Your dark demons illuminate your fiery gentleness
like the night sky shows off the stars.

To the dog in the dumpster and the pig in the water.

Dear dog in the dumpster,
Yours is the worst plight I've ever seen.
And I don't know what to do but weep for you
and the happy, hopeful way you wagged your tail.
I watch your pain through pixels and I pray to a God
I don't believe in.
"Send those men a merciless giant to crush their
souls and bones."
I'll remember your frightened face forever.
I will use the terror I know you suffered in those
seconds to fight with all I have to make a better
world for animals just like you.
For dogs both sweet and forcibly vicious.
I only wish it wasn't too late for you.
And I promise, though it offers you no comfort now,
that I'd take your place if I could.

Dear pig in the water,
I'm sorry that I could not make them stop.
That friendly hands were not around to take you from
your torture.
That you were born to people who value your flesh
above staving your fears.
That they see you as bacon or pork.
That the world is cruel.
Blind.
Greedy.
That you were one of the unlucky ones.
I wished you a fairytale much too late
and now you're nothing but faeces.
Your life was worth nothing more to the majority
than pounds
and pence.
And I promise, because it's all I can do now, that
I'll fight with all I have for your friends.

Gaslight.

Beat me over the head, love,
and spit out your bitter heart.
I'll root myself before you and bathe in scolding
words.

Scream your pain right at me, darling,
and writhe for strangers and friends.
I'll let you rive at me the way sad winds tear at
trees.

Shirk the blame, sweetheart,
and pretend you did not know.
I'll knit my lips and let you bask in endless,
splendid sympathy.

Shield yourself from the truth, babe,
and cast away your actions.
I'll help you knot your blindfold and whisper words
of woe.

Ignore my gentle actions, pet,
and the hopeful things I've done.
I'll help you tell the tallest tale two horrid
hearts can coin.

<u>Once upon a time in a girl.</u>

Your heart is a kingdom he longs to rule and you
call for him to save you,
flip your hair and sing your song and dance so that
he sees you,
but you already know that this ends with him cutting
off your head.
With dragons and poisons and wicked words.
It's all there in the fervent way he turns your
pages.
In the sword he brandishes shamelessly and the
gallant way he walks.
In the words that he speaks,
words you've heard before,
spoken to you by another boy,
in a bedroom,
some time long ago.

<u>To the man who loves me next.</u>

I am strong but I am scared.
Scarred.
Look closely and you'll see a path of tears etched
on my cheeks.

I am brave but I am afraid.
Affronted.
I never thought that love would happen to me ever
again.

I am firm but I am frightened.
And frightening.
You'll tell me I am more alive than anyone you've
known.

I am hopeful but I am wary.
Weary.
Many a bad man has enthralled me as vigorously as
you do.

I am curious but I am cautious.
Callous.
I won't believe those maple words you sing in the
beginning.

Know that I am yours.
Only yours.
And you'll never need another human for anything
again.

The land of hope and glory.

This is no land of hope and glory, it is a land of
blood and gore.
Where the men will be men and the women will accept
it and when you tell them the truth they'll
vehemently reject it because it's easier to pretend
that we are the best.
That we're life-savers and peace makers and not
blindfolded murderers.

But just because we're not there doesn't mean we're
not there.

Because it's our minds and our hands on the
landmines that tore up Iraq.
And our hearts in the bombs dropped each day on
Pakistan.
And our money and our votes that pay the wages of
the man who sells airplanes to Saudi so that they
can bomb Yemen.

So how are we better than the right-hand-raising
armies who killed six million Jewish people way back
when we stood for things we swear we still stand for
now?

How?

Tell me where is the hope and where is the glory in
the stories we have written in Britain?

Oh, mother!

We're bound together.
You and me.
Flowers and bees.
Trees and coyotes.
So it hurts my heart when we call rats pests, swat
spiders and wasps and take rabbits as 'pets'.
Race dogs and horses so we can bet on survival
and live as though we're immortal.

We're flooding the forests with fires and chainsaws
and emptying the ocean whilst filling the sea floor
with plastics and tampons and cigarette butts,
leaving mutts I the shelter to adopt 'proper' pups.
Ignoring brown and black babies and their
heartbroken mothers.
Telling transgender men that they can't be our
brothers and turning away from our struggling
sisters because they wear headscarves.

We laud the white man and screw everyone else.
Turn pigs into bacon and cows into belts.
Chase being skinny and eat through depression.
Blame strangers online for our own transgressions.
Stomp roads through woodland, rip oil from the
ground.
Throw our morals away when we're desperate for
pounds and pence.

We think we're a God we no longer believe in.
Take for granted the air that we breathe in.
Strangle ourselves with a rope that we made
whilst pumping our planet with polyphosphate.
Still we hold up our hands and ask why we're dying.
Why our Earth is crying with rage.
When with each fake frown,
each branch we pull down,

each hole we dig to fill with trash,
each pat on the back of a brazen, brash millionaire,
we forget that we won't get another chance.
That we are lucky to be here.

And whilst we only look after ourselves, we are
monsters to everything else.

www.ingramcontent.com/pod-product-compliance
Lightning Source LLC
Chambersburg PA
CBHW060550030426
42337CB00021B/4518